Victoriously with Prayer

The Dance Continues

BY: CYNTHIA E RAZO

A Global Dance of Faith, Every Story, Every Ability, One Victory.

From a blessing in disguise that began the testimony (Book 1), to thriving beyond the valley that deepened the journey (Book 2), and now rises into the dance that continues (Book 3). Your invitation to join this movement of faith begins here.

(También disponible en español / Also available in Spanish)

Cover design © 2025 by Cynthia E Razo, using licensed elements from Canva.com
ISBN (Paperback): 978-1-968083-12-0
ISBN (eBook): 978-1-968083-14-4
ISBN (audiobook): 978-1-968083-16-8
Published by Cynthia Razo Publishing
PrayerCoveredMe@gmail.com
This book is available in both English and Spanish editions
First Edition Printed in the United States of America
This work is a continuation of the testimony shared in Book 1, *Victorious Through the Power of Prayer –Breast Cancer: A True Blessing in Disguise,* and Book 2, *Victory Through Prayer – Thriving Beyond the Valley.* Together, these stories form an unfolding journey of faith, healing, and generational victory.

PRAISE FOR THE AUTHOR

A collection of words spoken by those moved, inspired, and strengthened by the life, testimony, and obedience of Cynthia E. Razo.

PRAISE FOR THE BOOK

Reflections from readers whose hearts were touched, whose faith was stirred, and whose steps found new rhythm within these pages.

ENDORSEMENTS

A testimony of impact from Books 1, 2, and 3, the dance of a story God continues to write.

Below are the expanded endorsements, including brand-new praise inspired by **Book 1** (*Victorious Through the Power of Prayer – Breast Cancer: A True Blessing in Disguise*) and **Book 2** (*Victory Through Prayer – Thriving Beyond the Valley*).

ENDORSEMENTS FROM BOOK 1

Victorious Through the Power of Prayer- Breast Cancer: A True Blessing in Disguise

"Her first book showed me that miracles don't just happen in hospitals, they happen in hearts that refuse to stop praying."

"Book 1 carried the raw weight of the valley, and yet every page was filled with courage. Cynthia taught us what it means to be held by God in the darkest places."

"I had never seen faith written with such honesty. This book made me believe again."

"Her testimony became the prayer I didn't know how to pray for myself."

ENDORSEMENTS FROM BOOK 2

Victory Through Prayer – Thriving Beyond the Valley

"Book 2 felt like breath, lighter, wiser, and overflowing with healing. Cynthia's voice matured, and her joy became contagious."

"In Book 2, Cynthia didn't just survive, she thrived, and she invited us to thrive with her."

"This book taught me that healing doesn't erase scars; it transforms them into testimonies."

"Every page felt like a gentle hand lifting me out of my own valley."

ENDORSEMENTS FOR BOOK 3

Victoriously With Prayer — The Dance Continues

"Book 3 carries a prophetic rhythm. It pulses with joy, restoration, and the sound of a woman who learned to dance again."

"This is more than a continuation, it's an elevation. Cynthia writes from overflow, not survival."

"Her chapters feel like worship. Her reflections feel like prayer. Her story feels like home."

"This is the book that will awaken joy in readers who forgot what joy feels like."

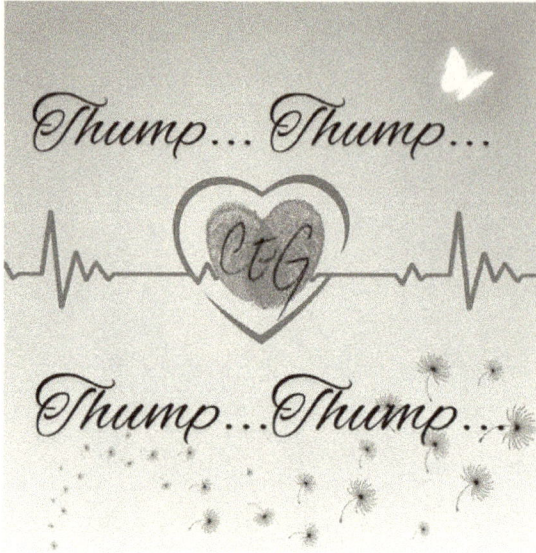

THE ORIGIN OF THE HEARTBEAT PROMISE

There are symbols that find us, not because we leave them behind, but because God writes them into our journey.

The pinky-print of Book 2 represented covenant, a promise between God and me, and a promise passed forward to every reader and listener. But as this third book was being birthed, another symbol emerged, quiet, steady, universal. One that belongs to every person, every ability, every age, every story.

The heartbeat.

A rhythm heard by the ear, felt by the hand, seen on a monitor, and carried in the spirit, even when the body cannot respond. The Heartbeat Promise is the evolution of the Pinky Promise:

a reminder that as long as the heart beats, even softly, even irregularly, even assisted, the dance continues.

For those who can move, and for those who cannot.
For those who can speak, and for those who cannot.
For those who can wiggle a finger, or blink, or breathe,
and for those whose bodies rest in hospital beds, yet whose spirits remain fully alive.

The heartbeat is God's signature on every life, and this promise is simple:

If your heart is still beating, your story is still dancing. Your victory is still in motion. God is not done. This is the meaning of the Heart-Wave Blessing. This is the seal of Book 3.

THE HEART-WAVE BLESSING
A Victory movement for Every Body, Every Ability, Every Breath. Before you step into this journey, pause with me. This is not a pause of silence; this is a pause of life. A pause of victory. A pause of presence. A pause where Heaven meets your heartbeat. Every one of us dances daily, whether we move or not. Every one of us carries a rhythm, thump… thump, until our very last breath, and that rhythm is worship. Is testimony. Is victory. Whether your dance is in footsteps, a lifted pinky, a head wobble, a wiggle, a breath, a blink, or complete stillness… Your life is still dancing.

God does not see the form. God does not see the limitation. God does not see the diagnosis. God sees the heart, and the heart is always in motion. Even in a hospital bed. Even in paralysis.

Even in coma. Even in silence. Even when the body cannot respond, the spirit can. That heartbeat, thump... thump...
is the universal choreography Heaven recognizes. You are included. You are covered. You are victorious.

THE HEART-WAVE BLESSING
1. The Pinky Lift, "I am Covered." If you can lift your pinky, lift it. If you cannot, feel it rise in your spirit. God sees your intention.
2. The Wave, "His Living Water Flows Through Me."
If you can wave your hand, wave it gently. If not, move whatever can move: a toe, a finger, a shoulder, your head.
If nothing can move, let your breath be the wave, and if breath is limited, let your spirit make the wave.
3. The Return to the Heart, "God Sees Me." Bring your hand, or your thought, your awareness, your spirit back to your heart. Feel the rhythm. Hear the thump... thump... That is your daily dance. That is your victory.

A SPIRITUAL MOMENT FOR EVERY ABILITY
Close your eyes or simply become aware. Notice your heartbeat or imagine it. Let your spirit breathe. Think silently:
"My heart dances. My spirit moves. I am victorious. I am covered in prayer."

THE DANCE CONTINUES...
In victory, with prayer, and for His glory. Side by side, heart to heart, every heartbeat, every soul, we will rejoice, testify,
and dance unashamed, victorious, and free. For the dance continues, in you, in me, in every thump, thump heartbeat God set in motion...and in every spirit He calls His own.

Dedication:

To my precious son, Gabriel, and my precious daughter,
Elizabeth, my heartbeat, my joy, and my greatest God-given
treasures. May the heartbeat on this cover remind you of the
truth I pray you carry forever: our hearts beat in sync when we
walk with God. Every thump… thump… you feel is a
reminder that you are never alone. God is always one prayer
away, one whisper near, one heartbeat present.
As your mother, I will love you until my last breath on this
earth…and for all of eternity in the presence of our God. I pray
you always know who you are, and more importantly, Whose
you are.
Walk boldly.
Pray continually.
Love deeply.
Dance freely.
Remember: your heart was created to beat in victory, never in
fear.
With all my love, always and for all eternity,
　　　Mommy

Acknowledgments:

With a heart overflowing with gratitude, I thank every soul who has chosen to take part in this miracle, near or far, known or unknown. Your prayers, your encouragement, your presence, and even the simple act of turning these pages have become part of this journey. **We all beat the same beat of love and hope, the very essence of this testimony.**

To the global community of all abilities, Blind, Deaf, Hard of Hearing, Nonverbal, Illiterate, and beyond, thank you for welcoming me, teaching me, and walking beside me. You have shown me that faith has no barriers and love has no limits. Together, we raise awareness, open doors, and remind the world that **every heartbeat matters, every voice matters, every story matters.**

To my precious children, Gabriel and Elizabeth, thank you for sharing your mommy with the world, for being patient, supportive, and full of grace during this God-given calling. You inspire every chapter I write and every seed I sow.

To my family, friends, and faithful prayer warriors, your prayers have strengthened me more than you know. Your love has carried me through valleys and helped me dance on mountaintops.

Above all…
To my Almighty God,
thank You for turning my mourning into dancing, my silence into testimony, and my heartbeat into a global movement of faith. **God is good. To Him be all the glory.**

Preface:

(Isaiah 61 : 1 NIV)

"The Spirit of the Lord is upon me, because He has anointed me to proclaim good news to the poor. He has sent me to heal the broken hearted, to proclaim freedom for the captives and release from darkness for the prisoners."

What began as a blessing in disguise became the doorway to everything that followed. Through that painful yet sacred season, God broke chains that reached far beyond the physical. He touched the deepest parts of me, emotionally, mentally, and spiritually, until every hidden bondage gave way to His power.

Through prayer, I overcame not only what was within me, but everything that surrounded me. Family, friends, strangers, even those I may never meet, were touched through the overflow of what God was doing. When prayer rises, it doesn't rise alone; it carries breakthrough, healing, and hope to everyone connected to it.

In my second book, *Victory Through Prayer: Thriving Beyond the Valley,* I learned that healing is not the end of the story; it's the beginning of unity. That book brought people together. It gave others a glimpse of what it means to walk through the valley, to go through the fire and not be burned. It reminded us that thriving isn't just about personal success, it's about inclusion: sharing your pain and your joy so that others may find strength to thrive.

Now, *Victoriously With Prayer*-the dance continues, continues that rhythm, a dance of empowerment and impact. It reveals how prayer in motion creates a domino effect of grace, how one act of faith can ripple through generations and nations.

This is the story of what happens when victory and prayer walk hand in hand, when faith moves from survival to song, from pain to purpose, from stillness to celebration.

the dance continues...

Reflection Moment

Take a moment. Take one gentle breath.
Let your heart slow into its natural rhythm, the rhythm God handcrafted for you.

Whisper softly:
"Lord, prepare my heart for what You want to reveal."

Scripture:

"Call to Me and I will answer you and tell you great and unsearchable things you do not know."
— Jeremiah 33:3 (NIV)

Prayer:

Heavenly Father, open my heart to receive, my mind to understand, and my spirit to hear Your whisper through these pages. Let this book meet me exactly where I am. Amen.

"Thump… thump… my heart says:"

- *"Lord, I am ready to learn…"*
- *"God, speak to me about…"*
- *"Today, I open my heart to…"*

These pages are for you, write, draw, pray, dream, and continue your own dance of victory.

Introduction:

(Matthew 18 : 19 – 20 NKJV)

"Again, I say to you that if two of you agree on earth concerning anything that they ask, it will be done for them by My Father in heaven. For where two or three gather in My Name, I am there in the midst of them."

When I first began this journey, I never imagined it would unfold into more than one book, yet here we are, three testimonies later, each one a new melody in the same song of faith.

The first book, *Victorious Through the Power of Prayer - Breast Cancer: A True Blessing in disguise,* was born from pain. It revealed how surrender unlocks miracles, how what looks like loss can become divine preparation. It was the story of how God took ashes and formed beauty, turning fear into faith and suffering into strength.

The second book, *Victory Through Prayer: Thriving Beyond the Valley,* was about walking out that faith, living it, sharing it, and inviting others to do the same. It was a bridge of inclusion, reminding the world that every story matters, every ability counts, and that thriving together means letting others see the fire you've survived and the grace that carried you through.

This third book, *Victoriously With Prayer – The Dance Continues,* is the celebration of all that has come from obedience and prayer. It's a reflection of what happens *after* the valley, when praise becomes the heartbeat of purpose.

Empowerment and impact are not separate from prayer; they are born from it. Every answered prayer creates a ripple, a movement of faith that travels beyond your immediate circle. United in prayer, we ignite the power of God.

This book is not just my story, it's a continuation of *our* story: a global testimony of what happens when people stand together in faith, lifting one another in love, compassion, and victory.

Prayer and victory have always been hand in hand, and when they move together, hearts are healed, lives are changed, and the dance of grace continues.

Reflection Moment

Place your hand over your heart.
Feel the steady *thump… thump…* This is your invitation into
the dance, God's dance of healing, strength, joy, and purpose.

Whisper:
"Lord, lead me in this dance."

Scripture:

"You turned my mourning into dancing."
— Psalm 30:11 (NIV)

Prayer:

**Heavenly Father, as I begin this journey, lead my steps,
steady my heart, and awaken the joy and healing You have
prepared for me. Let every page draw me closer to You.
Amen.**

"Thump… thump… my heart says:"

- *"God, take my hand in…"*
- *"Lord, guide my steps through…"*
- *"Today, I begin the dance of…"*

Write Your Thoughts

Table of Contents

Chapter 1: Opening Declaration- The Dance Continues: Living in Overflow

There comes a moment in every journey when God lifts your chin, steadies your breath, and whispers, *"This next step is overflow."* Not survival. Not recovery. **Overflow.** where survival turns into strength, strength turns into praise, and praise turns into a dance that cannot be silenced. As I opened my eyes to this new chapter of my life, I could feel it, a shift in the atmosphere, a widening in the spirit, a pull toward joy I could no longer deny. The dance that once began in a valley of tears now rises on a mountain of gratitude, and with every thump-thump of my heart, God reminds me:

"You are not just living... you are overflowing."

This book begins here, in motion, in worship, in testimony, where the dance continues, and the victory becomes your rhythm. That moment... is now.

I enter this third book not as the woman I was in Book One, broken, trembling, learning to trust God in the valley, and not even as the woman I became in Book Two, healing, rising, stepping into identity and purpose. I enter this book as a woman walking in overflow, a woman who has seen God's hand, felt His breath, heard His whisper, and experienced His victory in the deepest parts of her story.

This book is not written from survival. This book is not written from recovery. This book is written from freedom. From praise. From obedience. From an identity restored. From a heart that dares to dance before the Lord, unashamed, unafraid, and unbroken. The dance that David danced was not polished; it was powerful. It was not rehearsed; it was real. It was not for people; it was for God, and like David, I enter this book with boldness, with gratitude, with authority, and with a praise that comes from the depths of every valley I've walked through, and every victory God has carried me into.

This opening is not a beginning. It is a continuation, a declaration that the God who covered me in Book One and healed me in Book Two is the same God who now calls me to praise Him with my whole heart in Book Three. This book is my dance. My worship. My overflow. My offering, and may every page remind you of this truth:

If God brought you through the valley… He will teach you how to dance on the mountain. If God carried you in your weakness… He will ignite you in your strength. If God healed your heart… He will use your praise to heal others.

Let this book awaken the bold praise inside of you and stir the victory God already placed within you, because the story didn't end in the valley. The testimony didn't end in survival. The miracle didn't end in healing.

The dance continues…

"You turned my mourning into dancing; You removed my sackcloth and clothed me with joy." — *Psalm 30:11 (NIV)*

So, as this chapter sets the rhythm for the journey ahead, may you feel Heaven pulling you into new motion. Overflow is not a season you earn; it is a posture you receive. With every step forward, with every breath lifted toward God, may you discover that what once broke you now blesses you, what once drained you now fills you, and what once silenced you now sings. The dance continues, not because the valley is gone, but because God is with you in both the valley and the victory.

Reflection— Breathe in Strength

Take a deep breath.
Inhale God's strength. Exhale everything He never asked you to carry.

Scripture: Isaiah 40:29
"He gives strength to the weary and increases the power of the weak."

Prayer:
Lord, breathe Your strength into me today. Renew my courage and steady my heart. Amen.

Thump... thump... your heart says:

- *"God, equip me with..."*
- *"Lord, I surrender..."*
- *"Today, I receive strength for..."*

Write Your Thoughts

Opening Prayer

Heavenly Father,

as I begin this third book, I dedicate every word, every breath,
and every page to You.
Thank You for being the God of my valley, the God of my
healing, and the God of my victory.
May this book carry Your presence, Your joy, and Your
power into every heart that reads it.
Let it awaken praise, ignite hope, and release freedom.
Use this testimony for Your glory alone.
In Jesus' name,

Amen.

In victory, with prayer, and for His glory. **Thump… thump…**
For the dance continues…in you, in me, and across the world.

Before we step into the pages ahead, I want to meet you heart-to-heart, right here. You are not holding a book; you are holding a journey, one that pulses with grace, breathes with purpose, and beats with the love of a God who never left your side.

As you turn each page, may you feel welcomed, embraced, understood, and strengthened. My prayer is that you find yourself somewhere between the lines, in the whispers of hope, in the movement of faith, and in the gentle invitation to dance again. This is your safe space. Your sacred space. Your heart-to-heart with a God who hears every thump and treasures every breath.

When I began reflecting on the journey that brought me here, I realized that each book in this collection carried not only a message, but a *movement*. The first book, *Victorious Through the Power of Prayer -Breast Cancer: A True Blessing in Disguise,* was my valley, the testimony of survival and surrender. The second, *Victory Through Prayer: Thriving Beyond the Valley,* was my season of growth, proof that healing is more than recovery; it's transformation.

Now, *Victoriously With Prayer – The Dance Continues* represents the celebration, a rhythm of gratitude, movement, and praise. It is victory in motion.

"Victoriously" is not just a victory, it's a posture, a rhythm, a daily awareness of God's grace in motion. It speaks of living in God's grace. The word *With* reveals the secret of every triumph: *Prayer*. Through prayer, we move in harmony with God's will. We don't walk alone; we walk *with* Him. "With prayer" means a life that breathes with God, listens to God, and moves with God, and in that divine rhythm… *the dance continues.*

When I designed the cover, I asked God to show me an image that would speak to everyone, something that could be seen not just with the eyes, but with the heart. Thump…thump… the waves of the beating heart.

"Whoever drinks of the water that I shall give him will never thirst." *(John 4:14)*
That wave became the symbol of the *dance*, the rhythm of His Spirit moving across the world, carrying stories, healing, and hope to every shore.

The cover: a dance of faith across generations. Every one of my book covers has carried a piece of my journey, a visual testimony of where God found me, how He carried me, and where He is leading me. Book 3 is no different. In many ways, this cover is the most complete reflection of my past, my present, and the future God is still writing.

In Book 1, the butterfly reminded me of transformation, the beauty God creates from seasons of breaking. I didn't choose the butterfly… God placed it in my heart. It became a symbol of new breath, new hope, and a new beginning birthed from pain.

In Book 2, the dandelion seeds represented release, letting go, trusting God, and allowing Him to carry my testimony farther than I ever imagined. Each seed is a prayer, a whisper of hope, a moment of obedience scattered into the world. I learned that when God blows on your life, nothing stays small. Nothing stays local. Everything becomes global.

Now, in Book 3, everything comes together. At the center of this cover is a heartbeat line, steady, alive, and full of movement. It represents the rhythm of life God restored in me. But it also represents everyone: every story, every culture, every ability, every breath that joins this global dance of faith. This heartbeat is not just mine. It is ours. It belongs to the world God is gathering through this testimony.

Flowing from the heartbeat, the dandelion seeds continue to travel, carrying every victory, every testimony, and every promise God has fulfilled. They float across borders, languages, and generations, an ongoing reminder that faith moves, breathes, and reaches far beyond what we see.

Placed near the heart line is a symbol I hold close: my pinky-promise fingerprint heart. Inside it are the initials C • E • G — my children and me, our covenant, our legacy, our promise to God. It is the reminder that this assignment is bigger than a book. It is generational. It is sacred. It is a promise that the seeds I sow today will grow in the lives of those who come after me.

The butterfly (transformation), the dandelion seeds (release), the heartbeat (unity and life), and the pinky-promise heart (legacy and promise) now live together on this one cover.

This is my past, present, and future becoming one.

This Book 3 cover is not simply artwork. It is worship. It is testimony. It is remembrance. It is prophecy. It declares: A Global Dance of Faith, every story, every ability, one victory, and it invites you, with every heartbeat, to join the dance. This imagery speaks to the heart of what this book stands for:

inclusion, connection, and praise.

Each version of these books, whether spoken, printed, digital, large print, or braille, was created so that *everyone* can experience this story, regardless of ability. Why?, because testimony isn't meant to stay on a shelf; it's meant to be shared, heard, felt, and seen.

When I wrote my open-ended chapter at the end of the last book, I invited my readers and listeners to write *their* story, because the dance doesn't end with me. It continues through you. Every prayer, every victory, every act of courage adds another note to the melody of faith we create together. This book is the answer to that invitation. It reflects what has unfolded between *then* and *now*, a praise report of all that God has done, and all that He continues to do.

The dance continues. The story continues. The prayer continues.

Through it all, so does His grace

Victoriously With Prayer, is not just my next chapter, it's our collective praise report. As time passes, hourly, in days, weeks, months and even in years, the dance continues, stronger, freer, and more radiant than ever, because God's living water keeps us all in motion.

Time has passed since I first shared my journey through *Victorious Through the Power of Prayer -Breast Cancer- A true Blessing in Disguise* and *Victory Through Prayer: Thriving Beyond the Valley.* Each book carried a part of my testimony, one born in the valley, the other beyond it, and together they became a movement of faith, hope, and transformation.

Now, this new chapter carries a rhythm of celebration. *Victoriously With Prayer – The Dance Continues* is more than a title. It is a declaration, a continuation of praise, movement, and purpose.

In my first book, I reminded you that no matter what you face, physically, mentally, emotionally, or spiritually, *prayer is the key.* In my second book, I extended that truth with a pinky promise, a symbol of being covered in prayer from beginning to end. Now, time later, that same promise continues, but it has grown. It has traveled. It has danced.

This time, it moves with you, carried by the Living Water, reaching hearts across every ability, language, and nation. The pinky promise has become more than a gesture between author and reader.

It has become a living connection, a reminder that faith is still moving, prayer is still powerful, and victory is still being written. Just as a pinky promise cannot be broken, neither can God's Word. The same hand that held you in the valley now lifts you in victory. The same prayer that once covered you now calls you to dance, in faith, in freedom, in full surrender.

So as you begin this new chapter, remember:

The pinky promise continues with time, and beyond, you are still covered in prayer.

"You turned my mourning into dancing; You removed my sackcloth and clothed me with joy, that my heart may sing Your praises and not be silent. Lord my God, I will praise You forever."— Psalm 30 : 11–12 (NIV)

So before you turn the page, breathe. This book is not rushed; neither are you. You are stepping into a sacred conversation between your heart and God's heart. Let the words ahead hold you, guide you, stretch you, and strengthen you. May this heart-to-heart remind you that you are never alone, your pulse is known, your steps are ordered, and your dance is seen from Heaven.

In victory, with prayer, and for His glory. **Thump... thump...**

For the dance continues...in you, in me, and across the world.

Reflection—Hold your hands open.
Let them rest gently, as if receiving something sacred.
This is your invitation to meet God heart-to-heart.

Scripture:
Psalm 73:26 — "God is the strength of my heart and my portion forever."

Thump... thump... your heart says:

- "Lord, meet me in these pages..."
- "Help me hear You in my quiet places..."
- "Teach my heart to rest, trust, and receive..."

Write Your Thoughts

Some dances begin with music. But this dance, this holy, God-written dance, begins with a heartbeat. The cover of this book carries more than color; it carries revelation. It invites you to feel the rhythm God placed inside you long before you understood its purpose. Whether your heart beats strong, soft, steady, assisted, or by medical miracle, it still beats, and that beat is worship. This chapter brings you into the meaning behind the art, because the dance continues not just around you… but **inside** you.

The cover of *Victoriously With Prayer – The Dance Continues* carries a message that goes far beyond art, ink, and design. It is a living symbol, a heartbeat in motion, a testimony wrapped in color, light, identity, and praise. Every element was chosen to awaken something inside you, something eternal, something victorious. At the center flows the **heartbeat line**, pulsing boldly across the page. It represents the universal rhythm God placed inside every one of us, a rhythm that sings:
"You are alive. You are chosen. You are still dancing."

Some hearts beat naturally. Some beat with the help of pacemakers. Some beat through artificial hearts, machines, or medical miracles. But every heartbeat. whether soft, loud, steady, assisted, or mechanical, **is still a heartbeat allowed, sustained, and cherished by God.**

Through His divine wisdom, He gave doctors, scientists, and researchers the knowledge to create machines that sustain life, and because of that, **you too**, those with artificial hearts, repaired hearts, supported hearts, **you also have a dance.** A thump-thump... thump-thump... A rhythm of purpose. A global dance of 24/7 praise and worship.

Whether your heartbeat is:

- felt in your chest,
- heard through a monitor,
- seen on a screen,
- echoed through a device,
- or imagined in your spirit...

It is still worship.
It is still testimony.
It is still life in motion.

You are part of a worldwide rhythm of faith, from hospital beds and recovery rooms to living rooms, sanctuaries, workplaces, and silent private battles. Every heartbeat joins the same divine symphony. This is why the heartbeat crosses the cover, because it belongs to all of us. A holy reminder that **you are still here**, and because you are here... **your dance continues.**

The **fingerprint heart** symbolizes identity, your imprint in the world, your God-given purpose, your heritage, your legacy, and the covenant you carry: the Pinky Promise now evolved into the Heartbeat Promise.

The **butterfly** rises in motion with a glow, because transformation is not still, it is ever-moving, ever-growing, ever-dancing.

The **golden light** behind the heart represents glory, God's glory covering you, surrounding your story, and illuminating every chapter of your journey.

The **clear blue sky** reflects hope, clarity, and the breath of God, reminding you that your story is carried by the Living Water that strengthens, refreshes, and sustains.

This cover is not decoration. It is declaration. It declares that *every reader*, every listener, every survivor, every fighter, every person of every ability, those who walk, those who wheel, those who wiggle, those who blink, those whose bodies move freely and those whose bodies move silently, **all belong to the same dance. All are seen. All are victorious. All are held.**

When you look or visualize, this cover, let your heart say: **"My heartbeat is worship. My breath is testimony. My life is still in motion."** Let this cover whisper to you: **"Your dance did not end in the valley. Your praise did not stop in the fire. Your purpose is still beating, right now, inside you."**

As you hold this book, in whatever format and in your very own ability, feel it:

Thump-thump… Thump-thump… The dance continues, and so do you.

Reflection — The Rhythm of Life

Place your hand over your heart. Feel its steady beat. Whisper:
"Lord, thank You for this rhythm of life, of a heart learning to dance again."

Scripture: Acts 17:28
"In Him we live and move and have our being."

Prayer:

Father, thank You for sustaining me. Let each heartbeat remind me that You are not done with me. Let my life move in harmony with Your will. Amen.

Thump... thump... my heart says:

- *"God, thank You for..."*
- *"Lord, I trust You with..."*
- *"Today, I choose peace in..."*

In victory, with prayer, and for His glory. **Thump... thump...** For the dance continues...in you, in me, and across the world.

Write Your Thoughts

Chapter 4: The Testimony, The Vision: Where Purpose meets Pulse

Purpose does not arrive with a trumpet; it arrives with a whisper. A pulse. A divine stirring that tells your spirit, *"There is more."*

This chapter carries the faith that shaped my vision, the testimony that awakened my calling, and the pulse that reminded me God uses ordinary hearts to tell extraordinary stories. Every chapter of my life, and yours, beats with intention. Here, we follow the pulse of purpose until it becomes impossible to ignore.

As you have already read, and maybe even heard, I don't speak *religion*. I speak relationship with the great *I AM*... *God!* We all come from different backgrounds, and many hold different faiths. I genuinely honor and respect that. My heart is simply to pray for you, encourage you, and remind you that you are not alone. Don't give up. Don't lose hope. Most importantly, don't lose faith. There is undeniable power in prayer, and I am a walking, living testimony of that truth.

Life handed me lemons, and instead of becoming bitter, I chose to make lemonade and share it with the world. I choose to view every situation, circumstance, and obstacle through the lens of faith. Sometimes blessings are hidden beneath what looks like chaos, heartbreak, or disappointment. But let me tell you, God has a perfect plan and a perfect timeline. When we

surrender to His will, we step into alignment with His grace…
and He brings us through every valley.

When I completed my video testimony. in obedience, not
perfection, God opened doors I never imagined. That video
reached hearts I didn't even know were watching. Seeds of
hope began to blossom into faith. Lives were touched,
strengthened, redirected. Those who heard the message
became seed-carriers themselves, planting encouragement,
truth, and hope in the lives of others. This is how testimony
multiplies. This is how legacy spreads.

God also made a way for *inclusion* in this divine assignment.
He opened doors for my book to be available to the blind, to
those with dyslexia, and to individuals with visual
impairments through Bookshare. I donated my book, not for
profit, but for purpose. God, who sees the heart, blessed it and
multiplied it. When we do our part, He takes care of the rest.
This blessing in disguise is now reaching readers and listeners
around the world, igniting the fire of unity and prayer, the fire
that refines, not burns. I am rejoicing and dancing! Praise
God! Hallelujah! *The dance continues… through me, through
my children, and through you, my dear reader and listener.*

As Scripture reminds us:

> "Trust in the Lord with all your heart and lean not on your
> own understanding; in all your ways submit to Him, and He
> will make your paths straight."
> — *Proverbs 3:5–6 (NIV)*

This is the same trust God asked of Moses and the Israelites in the desert. God sent manna from heaven and instructed them to take only what was needed for the day. Why? Because He wanted them to learn to trust His daily provision, His perfect timing, His steady hand. That same God is with us now. He will provide. We simply take what is necessary, do what is ours to do, and watch Him multiply the rest.

Just like the young boy who brought the fish and the loaves, God took something small and created a miracle that fed a multitude. In that same way, God will equip you with every tool, every resource, and every ounce of strength needed for your divine calling.

This third book is more than pages; it is proof of the power of prayer. It is a reminder that God has given us victory, the kind of victory that makes us dance like David, with joy and freedom. This time, the dance is not just mine. It is a dance for my children, for your family, and for generations to come, so they, too, may witness and experience the boundless grace, faithfulness, and love of God.

The dance continues… and so does His glory.

Some seeds we won't see yet, as some blessings take days to bloom. Some take months, and some, like the seeds planted through obedience, take years. My Sister's house fire birthed the bold leap of faith towards my nephew's baptism, Their community joining forces and resources from across the country, the testimony, the Bookshare blessing… these are seeds God planted in the soil of our lives. Some have already broken through the ground. Others are still hidden, growing where we cannot see. Some will not be visible until God's appointed time, 3 years, 5 years, or even 7 years from now.

Purpose is not found in perfection; it is found in willingness. It is found in the quiet yes, the trembling yes, the faith-filled yes. As you move forward, may you pay attention to the divine pulse within you, the one that nudges, whispers, and leads you toward God-written assignments. Purpose doesn't shout; it beats, and when you learn to follow that beat, your whole life becomes a testimony in motion.

This next chapter is about learning to wait with expectation, trusting that God is cultivating something powerful beneath the surface. What we've lived so far is only the beginning. There is more to the dance. More miracles ahead. More testimonies unfolding.

Turn the page with faith. God is not done.

Reflection — A Heart Open to Healing

Place your hand over your chest.
Invite God into the places still tender, still healing. This is God saying: *Your life has intention.*

Scripture: Psalm 147:3
Jeremiah 29:11 — "For I know the plans I have for you..."

Prayer:
Heavenly Father, enter the places in me that still need Your touch. Heal me gently and completely. Amen.

Thump... thump... my heart says:

- *"God, heal this part of me..."*
- *"Lord, I'm ready to release..."*
- *"Today, I receive wholeness in..."*

In victory, with prayer, and for His glory. **Thump... thump...**
For the dance continues...in you, in me, and across the world.

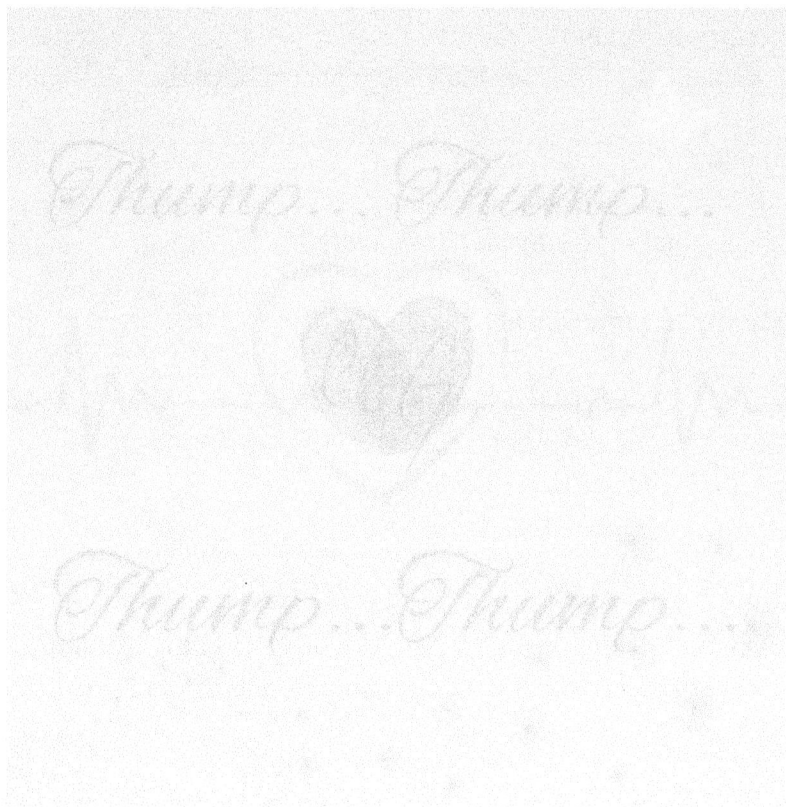

Chapter 5: Still Becoming: God's Transformation in the Waiting

Transformation is not loud. It is not rushed. It is not always seen. Most often, God does His deepest work in the waiting, in the quiet places where you wonder if anything is happening at all. But even in silence, the heart keeps beating, and God keeps shaping. This chapter is a testimony that becoming is a process, not a moment. A journey, not a destination, and even when you can't see it yet, God is forming beauty, strength, and purpose within you.

As I mentioned before, none of my books, videos, or audio projects were created by professionals. They were created by me, but truly, they were created through God in me.

He strengthened my mind. He guided my steps. He gave me the ability to self-publish every single format. Every time I prayed over a next step, He answered, above and beyond my asking. He poured out the knowledge, wisdom, courage, and skill I needed to complete each divine assignment He placed in my hands. But even after doing the work, there was a moment I found myself waiting, that quiet pause between obedience and outcome. That space where you wonder, "Lord... did I upload this right? Did I do my part? Will this reach who it needs to reach?"

It was in that honest, vulnerable wondering that God met me. As I prayed and chose once again to hand everything back to Him, to not let fear or uncertainty creep in, I took a deep breath, and in that breath, this is what I felt Him whisper to my spirit:

"Cynthia… that right there is pure faith, pure obedience, and pure peace. You have already done the part I asked of you. You released your testimony. You opened your hands. You shared your heart. You planted the seeds. Now you get to rest in the promise:

'One plants, another waters, but God gives the increase.'
— 1 Corinthians 3:7

Your video, your words, your books, they are already in motion. Even if people don't email. Even if they don't comment. Even if they never press 'like.' Even if they simply scroll quietly… Your voice is reaching places you cannot see. Your testimony is entering homes, routines, sickness, hope, and heartache. I am moving in ways that don't always show up on a screen. You didn't post for popularity; you posted for purpose. Purpose always produces fruit… sometimes silently… but always faithfully. I will bring the right people, at the right time, with the right hearts. You're not waiting alone. You're waiting with Me, and that makes all the difference."

That answer brought a smile to my face and a calm to my heart. In my spirit, I saw myself sitting next to God, side by side, not rushing, not striving, just resting, and He was smiling at me with such pride and tenderness, because He knows:

I trusted Him. I obeyed when it stretched me. I shared my story even when it cost me something. I walked through the valley and still chose faith. I released my testimony not for attention, but in obedience to purpose, and then, another whisper came:

"I'm still sitting beside you… admiring the courage of My daughter, the one who said yes, the one who walked through fire, the one who planted seeds that only Heaven can measure. No algorithm can define the impact you're about to make. No 'likes' can measure the souls you will reach. That smile you saw…that was Me saying: 'Daughter, I am pleased. You did exactly what I asked. Now… watch what I will do.' Take a deep breath. Stay seated beside Me. Let My joy cover you. I am already working behind the scenes, in hearts, in homes, in families, in quiet moments where your words will echo again and again."

So I waited, not empty-handed, not alone, but with God beside me. I took each day and made the best of it, even when some days felt more gray than sunny. Yet I remained seated in that holy place of stillness, letting God continue His work in me, because even in the waiting, He was still transforming me, strengthening me, shaping me, preparing me for the increase only He could bring.

So if you find yourself waiting, becoming, growing in unseen places, take heart. God does His finest craftsmanship in seasons with no spotlight. Even now, He is shaping you in ways that will surprise you later. Becoming is holy. Becoming is beautiful, and becoming is proof that God never stops writing your story, even in the quiet.

God is good — always. Today, He's still smiling at me and you..

Reflection — Strength in the Waiting

Sit still for a moment.
Imagine God standing beside you in the waiting.

Scripture says:

Isaiah 30:18
"The Lord longs to be gracious to you... He rises to show you compassion."

Prayer:
Lord, remind me that waiting is not wasting. Strengthen me as I wait on You. Amen.

Thump... thump... my heart says:

- *"God, I will wait for..."*
- *"Lord, meet me in this waiting..."*
- *"Today, I trust Your timing in..."*

In victory, with prayer, and for His glory. **Thump... thump...**
For the dance continues...in you, in me, and across the world.

Write Your Thoughts

Some moments are not planned; they are Heaven-orchestrated. That day, when I opened my mouth to speak, it wasn't me, it was the Spirit. It was Heaven pouring through a yielded heart. We often hear prayer requests, but not enough praise reports. We hear about battles, but not enough victories proclaimed aloud. This chapter invites you into a moment where God filled the sanctuary, revived faith, and rewrote hearts, reminding us that miracles still breathe, unity still calls down glory, and gratitude still opens the windows of Heaven.

God didn't just answer my prayers, He exceeded them. He went above and beyond anything I asked, imagined, or thought possible. He saw the quiet places of my heart, including the petitions I never spoke out loud, and responded with overflow. What He gave me was not just an answer… it was divine confirmation, multiplied grace, and a blessing far greater than my request. So today I boldly declare:

"With God, all things are possible." (Matthew 19:26)

"Enter His gates with thanksgiving and His courts with praise; give thanks to Him and bless His name."
— Psalm 100:4

With that truth sealed in my spirit, I walked forward not with fear or uncertainty, but with thanksgiving. Gratitude has become both my armor and my offering, the melody that carried me through the valley and now leads me into purpose and testimony.

I was invited to visit a sister church, a congregation who stood in the gap and prayed for me. Just as I did in New York, I felt the holy responsibility to publicly express my gratitude and give testimony of what God has done, because silence steals glory that belongs to Him. When God assigns intercessors, even from afar, gratitude becomes obedience and testimony becomes worship.

That day, nothing was scripted, it was Spirit-led. When I opened my mouth, Heaven filled the room. I realized something profound: We hear many *prayer requests*, but not enough *praise reports*. We hear of *battles*, but not enough *victories spoken aloud*. We hear of *storms*, but not enough *rainbows proclaimed*.

In that sanctuary, faith rose, hope awakened, and joy reignited. I didn't go to receive, yet I left overflowing. My cup was filled, and I know theirs were too, filled with peace, unity, expectation, and renewed faith that God still performs miracles. Prayer works. Unity invites glory, and gratitude keeps Heaven's windows open.

This journey is more than survival, it is assignment, mission, and legacy. The purpose behind my blessing in disguise is to thrive beyond the valley while helping others rise, heal, and dance toward their own victory. I must be clear: this was never done to gain wealth, recognition, or status, but to gain souls for God's Kingdom, to empower the weary, inspire the discouraged, and extend the very hand that once held me. If God carried me, I am determined to carry others. If He lifted me, I must lift others. We overcome *together*.

I am called, not by man, but by God. *I respond: "Here I am, Lord."*

I am chosen, not because I am perfect, but because He is faithful. *I respond: "Use me, Lord."*

I am sent, not to build my name, but to expand His Kingdom. *I respond: "For Your glory alone."*

Every valley becomes testimony. Every scar becomes evidence. Every breath becomes worship. *I respond:*

"Thy will be done."

As I left the church that day, after standing before the congregation to give my praise report, I felt something shift within me. There is a unique kind of healing that happens when we not only place our petitions before God, but when we return to give Him thanks publicly. Testimony completes the circle. Petition brings the need; praise reveals the miracle, and both are equally holy.

Sharing what God has done is not just a tradition, it is obedience. It is worship. It is our way of saying,

"Lord, I saw You. I acknowledge You, and I will not stay silent about Your goodness."

But what I didn't realize until that moment was that gratitude does not begin and end at the altar. It begins in the heart; it continues in our homes; it breathes through our words, our actions, our choices, and our daily walk.

Standing there, surrounded by the prayers that once carried me and the church family who interceded for me, I understood something deeper: **Thankfulness is not an event we visit. It is a lifestyle we live.**

As this chapter settles in your spirit, remember this: testimonies ignite faith, and praise carries power. Heaven moves when we speak of what God has done. May your life continue to declare the victories God has already written, both seen and unseen, spoken and unspoken. May every room you enter be filled with the same unscripted glory that once filled that sanctuary, reminding you... **we overcome together.**

That realization prepared my heart for the next chapter of this journey, a chapter not just about a season of gratitude, but about cultivating a **spirit of thanksgiving** that lasts all year long.

Reflection — A Moment of Abundance

Lift your chin slightly. As if looking toward Heaven.
Victory rises when praise rises. **Look around you.**
Name one blessing in the room, big or small.

Scripture: Psalm 23:5
"My cup overflows."

Prayer:
Thank You, Lord, for Your abundance. Help me to see blessings I often overlook. Amen.

Thump... thump... my heart says:

- *"God, I'm grateful for..."*
- *"Lord, You've blessed me with..."*
- *"Today, I recognize abundance in..."*

Write Your Thoughts

Thump... Thump...

Thump...Thump....

A Prayer of Gratitude & Overflow

Heavenly Father,
Thank You for Your presence that never leaves, Your power
that sustains, and Your love that heals the deepest places.
Thank You for going far beyond my requests, beyond my
understanding, and beyond what I dared to imagine.

Thank You for every person who prayed, interceded,
whispered my name before Your throne, and stood in faith
when I had no strength left. Bless them, Lord, multiply their
joy, deepen their faith, and surprise them with miracles.

Teach us to celebrate answered prayers as boldly as we
present new petitions.
May our lives never lack thanksgiving, obedience, or
testimony.
May unity remain our weapon, faith our anchor, and praise our
lifestyle.

Let our lives forever declare:
Prayer works. God is faithful, and with God, all things are
possible.
In Jesus' mighty and victorious name, Amen.

In victory, with prayer, and for His glory. **Thump... thump...**
For the dance continues...in you, in me, and across the world

Chapter 7: When Home Becomes An Alter

A house becomes a home when love fills it. But a home becomes an altar when **God** is invited to sit at the table. This year, hosting Thanksgiving was more than tradition, it was worship. Gratitude spilled into every corner, and a simple meal became a testimony in motion. This chapter reminds us that hospitality is holy, gratitude is a lifestyle, and every open door is a chance to reflect the heart of God. When home becomes an altar, joy becomes the fragrance, and love becomes the dance.

Today, I pause with a grateful heart. I am thankful and deeply honored that God chose me, and that I get to freely choose Him back. His goodness has carried me in the struggle and in the victory, in the quiet moments and in the joyful ones. God is good.

This year, God has blessed me with the opportunity to open my home and host Thanksgiving. It is more than a gathering; it is an altar of gratitude. I pray, declare, proclaim, and believe that there is always a seat at my table for God… and that each year after this one, my table will grow larger, not for the sake of numbers, but for the sake of honoring and glorifying Jesus.

But gratitude isn't seasonal. Hospitality shouldn't only bloom during the holidays. Every day is an opportunity to open our doors, our hands, and our hearts. There are people around us who may not need food on a plate, but nourishment for the soul, hope, grace, compassion, and the reminder that God still sees them.

This, too, is part of *dancing like David*. It is the rhythm of gratitude, the movement of obedience, the melody of joy that overflows until it touches others. We invite people to join our dance, and in return, God allows us to step into someone else's dance, their testimony, their healing, their breakthrough. God is God, yesterday, today, and tomorrow, and His presence moves through every shared moment.

> *Jesus taught us this kind of open-handed love:*
> *"For I was hungry and you gave Me something to eat..."*
> *(Matthew 25:35)*

We may never know when an angel stands among us, but we can always choose to be a blossom of hope for someone who needs it. A single act of kindness can grow into a garden of grace.

This Thanksgiving, I don't just give thanks, I give God room to move, and as long as I have breath, may my life continue to reflect gratitude, generosity, and a heart that dances before the Lord, unashamed and full of praise. Thump...Thump...

As the Thanksgiving season settled into my home and my heart, I found myself reflecting not only on the joy of hosting, but on the deeper meaning of gratitude itself. Gratitude is not just a holiday, it's a posture, a way of breathing, a daily surrender that opens our eyes to the blessings hidden in plain sight. The more I thanked God for what He had done, the more I realized how many of His greatest gifts had first arrived as **blessings in disguise**, wrapped in valleys, wrapped in trials, wrapped in tears that later watered the soil of my purpose, and just when I thought gratitude had finished its lesson, God revealed another layer: Gratitude doesn't only flow **from me** toward Him, sometimes it flows **back to me** through the voices of others, because as the year unfolded, the very people who read my book or watched my testimony began to speak life right back into me. Their words became confirmation. Their gratitude became mirrors of God's glory. Their messages reminded me that my obedience was never in vain, that God was using every part of my journey as a blessing for someone else.

That's when I understood:
The thanksgiving never ends.
The gratitude continues.
The testimonies are simply God's gentle way of saying,
"See... this is why I chose you."

As you close this chapter, may your home, no matter its size, style, or space, become a sanctuary of gratitude and grace. May your table become a place where heaven meets earth, where stories are shared, and where faith grows in the simple moments. Hospitality is worship, and gratitude is a daily rhythm. Let your home continue to echo God's presence, reminding you that every open door can lead to a miracle.

Reflection — The Dance of Joy

Smile intentionally.
Let joy rise, even if softly.

Scripture: Nehemiah 8:10
"The joy of the Lord is your strength."

Prayer:
Lord, place Your joy in my heart. Let it strengthen me and overflow from me. Joshua 24:15 — "As for me and my house, we will serve the Lord." *Amen.*

Thump... thump... my heart says:

- *"God, thank You for joy in..."*
- "Make my table a place of worship..." *"Today, my heart smiles because..."*

In victory, with prayer, and for His glory. **Thump... thump...**
For the dance continues...in you, in me, and across the world

Write Your Thoughts

Chapter 8: When their Words Became My Confirmation

Sometimes God sends confirmation through the mouths of others, a sentence, a whisper, a testimony that hits your spirit like lightning. This chapter holds the moments when God used people, conversations, and unexpected voices to remind me I was on the right path. Their words became anchors. Their stories became signposts. Their encouragement became wind in my sails. Here, you will see how God uses community to confirm calling and validate purpose.

There are moments in a calling where God allows the echo of your obedience to return to you, not as applause, but as confirmation. Not as praise, but as living fruit. In this season of my journey, the testimonies and messages from readers and viewers have become one of the most humbling gifts God has ever placed in my hands.

I never wrote for recognition.
I never recorded for validation.
I simply obeyed.

But obedience has a sound, and sometimes, that sound comes back in the voices of those whose lives God touches through your "yes."

Words that became mirrors of God's glory, as readers reached out and said:

"Cynthia, the words pop right out of the pages…"
It reminded me that God's Word, His living breath, can make anything come alive, even simple sentences written from a surrendered heart.

"Cynthia, I can totally hear your voice as I read this…"
That meant the testimony was true, authentic, unfiltered. It carried the same anointing in written form as it did when spoken.

"I took notes… I highlighted sections… these pages inspired me, moved me, and spoke directly to me…"
It reminded me that the Holy Spirit is the best highlighter. He knew which lines were meant to touch which hearts.

Then, about the video testimonies:

"Thank you for opening such a sacred, private moment and making it public…"
"You reminded me not to lose hope… my faith feels refreshed…"
"I can tell you opened your heart. I know God speaks through you."

Some offered no words at all. Just a smile… eyes glistening… a gentle sigh filled with relief, hope, and love.

Those silent responses spoke as loudly as the messages written to me.

It's overwhelming, in the best way, to witness God taking a small seed of obedience and watering it in the hearts of others.

A harvest I could never have imagined, there are enough messages, stories, and testimonies to fill an entire book of their own, and yet, every time someone says:

"Thank you."
I whisper back in my spirit:

"Thank You, God."

Why? because I am only the vessel.
A vessel who said yes.
A vessel who keeps saying yes.
A vessel who knows that the oil only flows when obedience is present.

Not my will, Lord, but Yours.

Every message, every testimony, every confirmation reminds me that the purpose is greater than the process, and the mission is bigger than the sacrifice.

It touched lives.
It healed hearts.
It refreshed faith.
It inspired hope.
It awakened prayer.

That alone makes every valley worth it.
Every tear worth it.
Every step worth it.

This is the dance,
a dance of gratitude.
In the valley.
On the mountain top, and everywhere in between. **God is good—Always.**

Just as scripture says:

"Let your light shine before others, that they may see your good deeds and glorify your Father in heaven."
— Matthew 5:16 (NIV)

"And whatever you do, whether in word or deed, do it all in the name of the Lord Jesus, giving thanks to God the Father through Him."
— Colossians 3:17 (NIV)

"You are my witnesses," declares the Lord, "and My servant whom I have chosen…"
— Isaiah 43:10 (NIV)

But perhaps some of the most unexpected testimonies came in ways I never imagined through the very journey that once brought me to my knees. I remember the day I looked at my doctor and said with complete certainty:

"Someone is going to go through this, and I need to go through it so I can help them. What better way to truly help than to understand it myself, so that I know what to say, what to do, and how to walk with them?"

At that time, I believed *I* needed to experience it in order to help others. But now, standing on the other side with clarity in my spirit, I realize something deeper:

They never really needed **me**.
They needed **God**.

God spoke through me.
God comforted through me.
God encouraged through me.
God poured strength, wisdom, and love **through** a vessel that simply said "Yes, Lord, and now I understand why.

Because today, I am asked questions I never expected:

"Cynthia, my friend is starting chemo… how can I help her?"
"What can I buy for someone who's about to go into surgery?"
"Cynthia, would you be willing to speak encouragement over my cousin, my sister, my coworker…?"

Every time someone asks, I am reminded:

This was never about my suffering. This was about my **assignment**. It was never about my strength. It was God's strength flowing through me. So, I take no credit, not one ounce. I cannot. I will not.

All I know is this:
The love God poured into me…
The courage He dressed me with…

The peace He wrapped around me…
The wisdom He whispered into me…

I now give it away freely, joyfully, lovingly.

Not *regifting*,
But **overflowing** what God gave abundantly.

The same way manna fell from heaven, just enough for each
day, God gave me exactly what I needed for my valley, and
now He uses that same portion to nourish others in theirs. This
is why I have reached out to leaders in my support groups…
to my medical team… to the community around me… because
there is a need that is greater than medicine alone, a need for
faith-based support, for prayer-filled strength, for
encouragement anchored in God's promises, and I am ready.
Ready to stand in the gap.
Ready to serve.
Ready to speak life.
Ready to be part of a faith-rooted support group where God is
welcomed in, honored, and glorified, because with God, all
things are possible, and truly, **God works in mysterious,
intentional, beautiful ways.**

He goes before us.
He prepares the path.
He equips us long before we ever understand why.

He gives favor… and then teaches us what to do with it, and
now, I stand in awe because I can see the full circle: What the
enemy meant for harm, God turned into ministry. Into
purpose. Into compassion. Into a calling stronger than fear

itself, and this, too, is part of the dance.

A dance of obedience.

A dance of gratitude.

A dance of purpose.

A dance of healing, for me and for others.

> *"Praise be to the God... who comforts us in all our troubles, so that we can comfort those in any trouble with the comfort we ourselves receive from God."*— **2 Corinthians 1:3–4 (NIV)**

> *"The Lord goes before you and will be with you; He will never leave you nor forsake you."* — **Deuteronomy 31:8 (NIV)**

When God speaks through others, He is not just confirming direction, He is confirming identity. Let every affirmation, every testimony, every Spirit-led word continue to shape you into boldness and obedience. As you move forward, may you stay sensitive to God's confirmations, both loud and soft, knowing He's guiding your steps and sending the right voices at the right time.

Take one step forward. (physically or in you ability)
A prophetic gesture of moving with God.

Scripture: Psalm 119:105
"Your word is a lamp to my feet."

Prayer:
Lord, guide my next step. Align my walk with Yours. Amen.

Thump... thump... my heart says:

- *"God, lead me into..."*
- *"Lord, I will take the step toward..."*
- *"God, help me recognize Your voice..."*

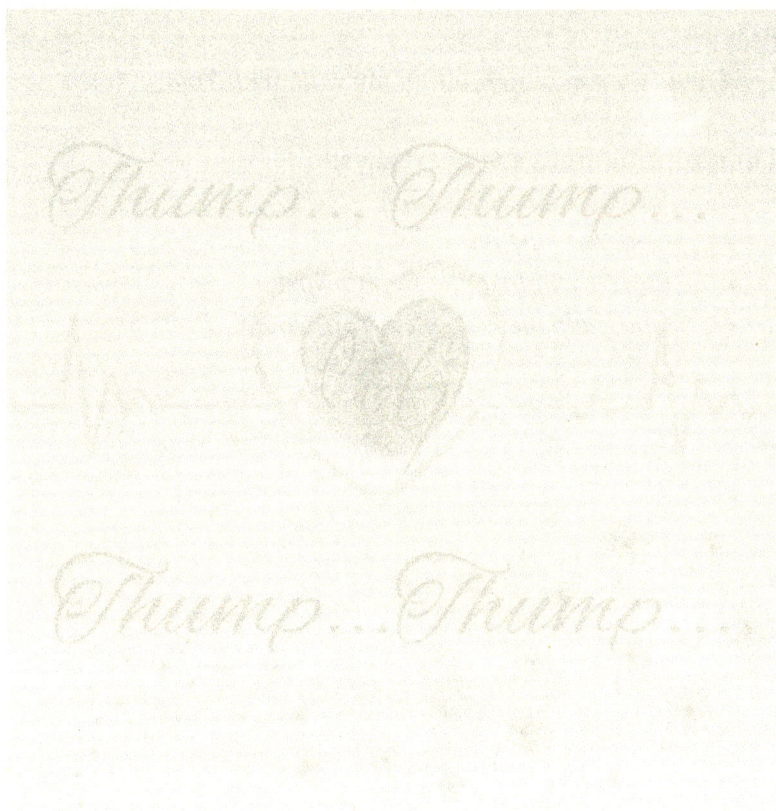

Write Your Thoughts

Prayer of Gratitude

Heavenly Father,
Thank You for turning my valley into a vessel.
Thank You for allowing my story to become comfort for
others,
not by my strength but by Yours alone.
Thank You for every person You send my way,
those who need encouragement, hope, prayer, or simply
someone who understands.
Equip me daily with Your wisdom, compassion, and grace.
Let every word I speak be Your voice.
Let every act of love reflect Your heart.
May the overflow of what You poured into me continue to
touch every life You place before me.
To You be all the honor, all the glory, and all the praise.
In Jesus' mighty name,

Amen.

In victory, with prayer, and for His glory. **Thump... thump...**
For the dance continues...in you, in me, and across the world.

The power of prayer is woven through my story, my healing, my identity, and my legacy. It is the thread that ties generations together and the wind that keeps the dance alive. This chapter celebrates the prayers that carried me, the intercessors who stood for me, and the legacy that continues to ripple outward, one heartbeat at a time.

Before every victory, there is a prayer. Before every celebration, there is a cry from the heart that God turns into a testimony. This chapter is the doorway into the miracles that are still unfolding… including the one you will read next.

There is power in prayer. Not symbolic power. Not poetic power. **Real, life-changing, mountain-moving power.**

I say it again: **prayer is powerful**.

Prayer is not a ritual, it is a lifeline. It is the quiet surrender that says, *"God, I trust You."* It is the whispered cry that reaches Heaven before it ever leaves our lips. It is the dance between our human need and God's divine response.

Throughout Scripture, women and men prayed, and God answered. Not always instantly. Not always the way they expected. But *always* with purpose, and *always* with victory.

These stories remind us that **prayer does not expire, weaken, or age**. The same God who heard them hears us. The same

God who moved then is moving now. The same God who delivered then is delivering today.

Praying Women of the Old Testament

Hannah, A Prayer in Deep Pain Barren. Heartbroken. Misunderstood. Yet she poured out her soul, and God gave her Samuel, the prophet who shifted a nation.
"For this child I prayed…" — 1 Samuel 1:27

Esther, A Prayer That Required Courage. A queen with trembling knees but a steady faith. Her prayer empowered her to stand before a king and save her people.
"For such a time as this." — Esther 4:14

Deborah, A Prayer for Victory A judge. A prophet. A warrior. She prayed for God's strategy and watched Him deliver Israel.
"March on, my soul; be strong!" — *Judges 5:21*

Sarah, A Prayer in the Waiting Years of delay. Years of confusion. Yet God fulfilled His promise with Isaac, proof that no season is too late.
"Is anything too hard for the Lord?" — *Genesis 18:14*

Abigail, A Prayer for Protection. Her wisdom and prayer prevented bloodshed and saved her entire household.
"Blessed be your discernment." — *1 Samuel 25:33*

Praying Women of the New Testament

The Woman with the Issue of Blood, A Prayer of Faith One touch. One act of courage. Jesus called her "daughter" and

healed her.
"Your faith has made you well." — *Mark 5:34*

The Canaanite Woman, A Prayer That Refused to Give Up.
Her persistence released her daughter's miracle.
"Woman, you have great faith!" — *Matthew 15:28*

Mary, Mother of Jesus. A Prayer of Surrender. Her response
changed history:
"Let it be to me according to Your word." — *Luke 1:38*

Anna, A Prayer That Endured. Decades of fasting, worship,
and prayer… and she lived to see the Messiah with her own
eyes.
"She never left the temple, praying night and day." —
Luke 2:37

A Man Whose Prayer Shook the Earth. Joshua, A Prayer for
the Impossible He asked God to make the sun stand still, and
God did.
"The sun stopped in the middle of the sky." — *Joshua
10:13*

One God. One Story. One Faith That Continues to Dance. The
prayers of the Bible are not ancient stories… they are
testimonies of *who God still is.*

Their dance of faith becomes our dance. Their courage
becomes our inheritance. Their boldness becomes our
reminder that prayer is not powerless, **it is victorious**, because

*God is the same **yesterday, today, and forever** (Hebrews 13:8).*

He answered then.
He answers now.
He will answer for generations yet to come.

**The dance continues...
and so does the power of prayer.**

As this chapter comes to a gentle close, may you never underestimate the power of a praying heart. Prayers don't expire; they echo through generations. They outlive seasons, storms, and struggles. They carry victory into places we may never walk ourselves. Let your own legacy of prayer continue to dance long after your words fade, because every prayer becomes part of Heaven's story over your life.

As you turn the page, you will step into a glimpse of what happens when years of prayer, surrender, faith, and obedience collide with God's perfect timing. The celebration you are about to read is more than a *future moment;* it is the harvest of every prayer ever whispered.

A Prayer

Heavenly Father,
**Thank You for the legacy of faith woven through
Scripture.
Thank You that every story of answered prayer
reminds us that You are faithful, present, and unchanging.**

Give us the boldness of Deborah,
the courage of Esther,
the perseverance of Hannah,
the trust of Sarah,
the discernment of Abigail,
the faith of the woman who touched Your garment,
the persistence of the Canaanite mother,
the surrender of Mary,
the endurance of Anna,
and the confidence of Joshua.

Teach us to pray with expectation,
to wait with hope,
to move with faith,
and to live in victory.

May our lives become a testimony
that prayer is powerful and God is faithful.

In Jesus' mighty name,

Amen.

In victory, with prayer, and for His glory. **Thump… thump…**
For the dance continues…in you, in me, and across the world.

REFLECTION — *Prayer That Moves Mountains*

Place your hands together gently,
as if cradling your own prayer.
Feel the warmth.
Feel the nearness.
Feel God holding you as you hold Him.

Scripture

"The prayer of a righteous person is powerful and
effective."
— *James 5:16*

Prayer

Father, strengthen my faith.
Teach me to pray without fear, without doubt, and without
hesitation.
Let every prayer I lift rise with trust and land with victory.
Amen.

Thump… thump… my heart says:

"Lord, deepen my prayer life…"

"Let my prayers touch generations…"

"Teach my spirit to intercede with boldness…"

Write Your Thoughts

There is a promise in my spirit, a Saturday marked by God, sealed with victory, and waiting for its appointed time. This chapter is a declaration in advance, a prophetic whisper that tells my heart: *"You will dance again on that day, stronger than before, with a testimony only Heaven could write."* Here, I sow the promise. I speak the prophecy. I declare the pulse of a future victory that is already beating in the hands of God.

What you are about to step into is not imagination, it is expectation. A holy whisper of what God is shaping behind the scenes, woven from every prayer, every tear, every surrender, every thump-thump of faith.

I looked ahead out of curiosity... and there it was.

2030. Seven years later. A Saturday.

The same day of the week as my first-year surgery, my anniversary, also a Saturday. I felt it in my spirit immediately. A whisper, soft but certain, brushed through me:

> *"Oh, Cynthia... this is Me. This is My alignment. My signature. My promise."*

Chills ran through me, the holy kind. Seven... God's number of divine completion, wholeness, and covenant, and Saturday... the day God Himself set aside for rest, reflection, joy, and looking back at all He made and calling it *good*. No coincidence. Just confirmation.

My first anniversary was thanksgiving, a sigh of relief, a hallelujah whispered through healing. I celebrated that 1st anniversary with my children, my family and my Prayer Warriors. My seventh will be completion and rejoicing, the full dance of victory. The moment where my story, my faith, and my pinky-promise legacy converge.

I proclaim it.
I declare it.
I believe it.
I receive it.

A glimpse into a future God has already seen…

I imagine… and I pray…

"Seven years later, on another Saturday, I stood in the same light, healed, whole, and still dancing. The day of rest had become a day of rejoicing. What began as survival became celebration. The pinky promise continues… and so does His faithfulness."

Every year before it was victory. Every year after it will be praise, and God, who knows the desires of my heart, will surpass even the things I dare to imagine.

The Scene, Step into the Room with Me…

The morning light felt familiar. Warm. Gentle. Alive with promise, as if God kissed the sky before I opened my eyes. Seven years had passed since the surgery that changed everything… Yet as I stood in that doorway, it felt as though time folded in on itself. The same sun that rose over my valley now shined over my victory. It was Saturday again the day God crafted for rest since the beginning. The day He whispered once:

"Be still and know that I am God."

But today, the stillness carried a rhythm.

Thump… Thump…

The heartbeat became a rhythm. The rhythm became a dance. I stepped outside and felt the air, soft, fragrant with rain and sunlight, like heaven was only one breath away. A butterfly drifted by… wings opening like a quiet hallelujah.

Dandelion seeds rose into the breeze, tiny white prayers carried into places I may never walk, and then, without even thinking, my right hand lifted. My pinky finger traced the air, the same movement I've made so many times, then rested over my heart.

"Lord, we did it again.
Seven years later…
and I'm still dancing with You."

There was no stage. No music. No crowd. Only God, and that was enough. The God who met me in the valley now danced

88

with me on the mountain. The prayer that once covered me now flowed through me, and this dance, this seventh-year praise, no longer belonged to me alone.

It belonged to *everyone* who prayed, believed, cried, hoped, walked, or witnessed this journey,:

Readers.
Listeners.
Warriors.
Survivors.
Dreamers.
Hope-carriers.

We were all moving together in the same rhythm of grace. Thump…Thump…

Seven years later. Same day. Same God. Same faithfulness. Now, this promise rests in God's hands, sure, steady, and sealed. What He has spoken, He will fulfill. The prophetic Saturday you carry in your spirit is not fantasy; it is faith. Not imagination; but revelation. May this promise beat louder in your heart with every passing day, reminding you that victory has a pulse… and your story has a chapter still unfolding.

2030 will mark seven years. After that… only God knows the year He calls me home.

But until then, I will celebrate every year, Every breath, Every mercy, Every heartbeat…

Thump…Thump… The dance continues…

Reflection — The Miracle of Today

Lift your eyes upward.
Acknowledge the gift of this very moment. **Lay your palm over your heart.**
Speak the promise aloud, even softly.
Prophecy begins in the pulse.

Scripture: Psalm 118:24
"This is the day the Lord has made; let us rejoice and be glad in it."

Prayer:
Father, thank You for today. Help me see this day as a miracle and an invitation to walk with You. Amen.

Thump... thump... my heart says:

- *"God, I rejoice in..."*
- *"Lord, thank You for today's..."*
- *"Today, I celebrate..."*

Write Your Thoughts

Closing Prayer: "The Dance Continues"

Heavenly Father,
Thank You for every valley You carried me through
and every mountain You called me to climb.
Thank You for turning pain into purpose,
tears into testimony,
and silence into song.

On this seventh Saturday, I lift my praise to You,
not for the things I see,
but for the things You've yet to reveal.
You are the rhythm of every heartbeat,
the melody in every prayer,
the living water that keeps my soul in motion.

Let this dance never end,
not in my life, not in theirs.
May every story birthed from this journey
carry Your light into places my feet may never go.

In every breath, every step, every note of faith,
let the world see the beauty of Your grace,
alive, moving, and victorious.

In Jesus' name,
Amen.

In victory, with prayer, and for His glory. **Thump… thump…**
For the dance continues…in you, in me, and across the world.

As this epilogue closes, know this: **the dance does not end, it evolves.** You are stepping into a new season of joy-led obedience, Spirit-led purpose, and victory-led living. Let joy be your rhythm now. Let gratitude be your melody. Let worship be your motion. **The dance continues... in freedom, in victory, in joy.**

Every story has an ending, but not every ending dances. This epilogue is not a closing; it is a continuation, a joyful bow, a grateful inhale, a praise-filled exhale. Joy has become my rhythm, and worship has become my motion. As this book comes to a close, the dance does not stop. It simply shifts into a brighter, stronger, deeper celebration of who God is and who I am becoming in Him.

Before you turn this page, take one breath and one truth with you:

Your story isn't finished, and neither is mine.

This book may be closing, but the growth continues, quietly, faithfully, beautifully. The chapters may end, but God does not. If the final chapter showed you the *dance*, this epilogue will show you the *meaning* behind the dance, the why, the how, and the gentle lessons God whispered in the spaces between victory and becoming.

This is where I step back, look at the journey with you, and say:

Look what God has done…and look what He is still doing.

Let's turn the page together. Every season of my journey has carried its own weight. Book One carried the heaviness of the valley. Book Two carried the breath that followed the valley. But Book Three… Book Three carries something different. It carries **joy**, pure, undeniable, God-given joy.

When I held the first proof of this book in my hands, it was light. Not just in pages, but in spirit, and God whispered to me again:

"This is what joy feels like."

This time, the pages didn't feel like battle or even survival. They didn't feel like learning how to stand, how to breathe, or how to heal. This time, the pages felt like **movement**, like a gentle sway, like a lifted hand, like a heart *learning how to dance again*, because this season wasn't about endurance. It wasn't about recovery. It wasn't even about rebuilding. This season was about **celebrating what God has already restored.**

Book One was the cry.
Book Two was the breath.
Book Three is the **dance**.

Something beautiful happened while writing this book… My voice changed. Not because of technique or training, but because the *weight* of the testimony shifted. The God who walked with me through diagnosis, the God who carried me through treatment, the God who strengthened me through healing, is the same God who now invites me to dance with Him. With every chapter, every reflection, every prayer, I realized my heartbeat wasn't the same either.

In Book One, my heartbeat was trembling.
In Book Two, my heartbeat was steady.
In Book Three, my heartbeat is **dancing**,
freely, boldly, globally.

That is why this book had to be light. Joy is light. Praise is light. Freedom is light. Dancing with God cannot be heavy, because He carries the weight, and we carry the worship.

Now, as this book closes, a new truth stands before me:
I am not the woman from Book One.
I am not even the woman from Book Two.
I am the woman God shaped **through** the valley, and the woman He taught to **dance** beyond it.

What began as survival… became healing… and now has become **celebration**. This celebration is not mine alone.

It is global.
Every story.
Every ability.
Every culture.
Every breath.
Every heartbeat.
A dance of faith woven together across the world.

So, with gratitude overflowing, and with the same heartbeat that carried me from page one, I close this book with the declaration God wrote on my spirit long before I wrote a single chapter:

The dance continues… in me, in you, and across the world.

A readers and listeners blessing: a blessing for the one who dances with God.

May the God who carried you through every valley now teach your feet to dance upon every promise.

May your heart beat softly in His presence, and boldly in His calling. May each thump… thump… remind you that you are never alone, for your heartbeat is held by the One who spoke life into you before time began.

May joy rise where sorrow once lived. May hope bloom where fear once whispered. May strength awaken where weariness once lingered and may the peace of God surround you like a melody only heaven can compose.

I bless your steps, that they move with courage and grace.

I bless your voice, that it carries truth, healing, and praise.

I bless your spirit, that it shines with the light only God can give.

I bless your journey, that it becomes a testimony of faith, resilience, and love, and as you go forward, beloved reader, listener, may you always remember:

Your story is part of the global dance of faith.
Your heartbeat has purpose.
Your praise has power.
Your life carries victory.

May God go before you; God stand beside you, God dwell within you, and God dance with you for all the days of your life. **Amen.**

As the final words settle into your spirit, may joy become more than an emotion, may it become your movement. Joy is the dance that cannot be stolen, the praise that cannot be silenced, and the heartbeat that carries you into every new season. This isn't goodbye; this is a new beginning. Joy has taken the lead, and your dance with God continues.

Epilogue Reflection: As the Dance Continues

Before you close this book, take a moment with me,
a sacred pause, a breath of gratitude, a final dance step with
God.

Wrap your arms around yourself, the same way God has
wrapped His arms around you through every valley, every
victory, every quiet moment, every unseen miracle.

Feel His covering. Feel His nearness. Feel His wings over
your life, steady, warm, protective, loving.

Now, **place your hand gently over your stomach.**
Feel your breath rise… and fall. Let each inhale remind you:

God is not finished with you.

Let each exhale release the last residue of fear, doubt, or
hesitation, because this epilogue is not an ending, it is an
opening. A gentle doorway into the next chapter of your life,
your testimony,
your ministry,
your dance.

You are now standing in a place where **God's covering meets
God's courage.** A place where **His wings shelter you, and
His strength rises inside you.** A place where the dance
continues. As scripture declares:

"He will cover you with His feathers,
and under His wings you will find refuge."
— *Psalm 91:4*

"Be strong and courageous…
for the Lord your God is with you wherever you go."
— *Joshua 1:9* Amen.

A Heartbeat: Final Invitation

As you step into your next God-written chapter, let your heart speak:

"Thump... thump... my heart says:"

- *"God, I feel Your covering over..."*
- *"Lord, thank You for protecting..."*
- *"Today, I rest under Your wings in..."*
- *"God, give me courage to..."*
- *"Lord, help me face..."*
- *"Today, I choose bravery in..."*

Write Your Thoughts

Final Closing Prayer:

A Prayer to Activate the Dance Within You

Father God,
I come before You with a heart full of gratitude for the one
who reads and listens to these pages, the one You chose, the
one You called, the one You lovingly drew into this dance of
faith.

Today, Lord, I ask for activation.
Activate their joy.
Activate their voice.
Activate their courage.
Activate their gifts,
the ones You placed in them long before they were born.

Let every dormant dream awaken.
Let every weary part be restored.
Let every heavy burden lift.
Let every fear bow to Your name.

Lord, with Your mighty hands, touch their heart right now,
and let them feel **Your heartbeat in theirs.** Let them sense
the **thump... thump...** that reminds them You are near, You
are present, and You are guiding every step.

Ignite in them a holy fire to pray without fear, to worship
without shame, to testify without hesitation, and to walk
boldly into the purpose You crafted just for them.

Let their life become a moving, breathing declaration of Your goodness.

As this book closes, may a new chapter begin, one filled with joy, movement, healing, and the unshakable truth that:

The dance continues...
in them, through them, and far beyond them.

We ask, We believe, we receive, In the powerful, victorious name of Jesus,
Amen.

In victory, with prayer, and for His glory. **Thump... thump...** For the dance continues...in you, in me, and across the world.

To God be the Glory.

The dance continues... As joy takes the lead and the dance continues into new seasons, there is one more revelation God whispered into my spirit, a final chapter that completes this book with divine purpose. Just as the disciples walked with Jesus, twelve steps complete a journey, and before this testimony closes, God reminded me of one last truth: **some victories don't come from fighting... they come from praising.** So, we arrive at Jericho, not as spectators, but as dancers in God's victory.

Chapter 12 The Jericho Dance: When Praise Breaks Barriers

Twelve.

A number God has woven throughout Scripture, a number of completion, authority, and divine order.

Twelve tribes.
Twelve gates.
Twelve stones of remembrance.
Twelve disciples who carried the message forward, and now...
twelve chapters.

This book does not end at twelve by coincidence, but by **assignment**, because this testimony is not just about surviving seasons; it is about walking in **spiritual governance**, authority in identity, and the divine order God has set over your journey and mine.

Twelve chapters seal this book the way twelve disciples sealed a movement. This is completion with purpose. As this final chapter settles into your spirit, **may joy take the lead in your steps.** Joy that flows without force. Joy that rises without explanation. Joy that dances even when the music is silent.

This joy is not fragile, it is fortified by everything God has brought you through.

Your heart has learned to beat again. Your faith has learned to rise again. Your spirit has learned to **dance again**.

Some battles are not won by strength, strategy, or striving, they are won through **obedience, movement, and praise.** The story of Jericho is not simply a miracle of fallen walls; it is the **revelation** of what happens when faith marches and praise leads the way.

The Israelites didn't shout because the walls fell. **The walls fell because they shouted.** In the same way, your praise carries weight. Your worship carries authority. Your obedience carries spiritual force. Before breakthrough ever appears, your heartbeat already carries a rhythm Heaven recognizes: the rhythm of a believer who has chosen trust over fear.

Some walls fall instantly. Others fall in stages. But **every wall falls** when God says it must. The Israelites walked seven times around their "impossible." Seven, the number of completion. Each lap was a declaration:

"We trust You even when we don't see movement."

So, when the seventh lap came, when they lifted their voices in unified praise, Heaven responded. The walls didn't simply crack. They **collapsed** under the weight of God's promise. This... is your **Jericho dance**. Not a dance of perfection, but of **persistence**. Not a dance of performance, but of **praise**.

With every heartbeat…thump-thump…with every prayer whispered in faith, with every breath of surrender, you declare:

**"God, I will do my part…
and You will take care of the rest."**

Let this settle deeply in your spirit:

You are *Victoriously… with prayer.* You are *dancing in faith.* Your daily thump-thump is breaking barriers you don't even see yet.

As I stepped into this chapter, my **Jericho season**, I realized something powerful:

Praise is not always a whisper. Sometimes it is a **shout**. Sometimes it is the sound that makes the walls crumble. Sometimes it is the moment Heaven says:

"Now… sing."

Just as the Israelites marched around their walls, as I marched through my valleys, my treatments, my surgeries, my fears, and my victories, a melody began to rise inside my spirit.

At first soft. Then steady. Then unstoppable.

I am not a professional singer. I am a worshipper. A daughter. A Warrior. A testimony, and in this Jericho moment of my journey, **God allowed my heart to become a song, a Psalm.**

Through prayer, I birthed a worship song straight from my valleys, my battles, and my testimonies.

This is not just a song. This is my **shout**. This is my **wall-falling moment**. This is my **victory dance**.

Below are the lyrics gracefully crafted, a worship offering born from my depths and risen into praise.

My Jericho Song: The Sound Of My Shout

Aleluya.
You are the Alpha and the Omega.
With a grateful heart, I come before You
with thanksgiving
and a dance of praise.

You held me when fear surrounded me,
when night outlasted the promise of morning.
You carried my breath when my strength was thin
and whispered hope when my voice fell silent.

Before I faced the valley,
You were already at work in my mother's womb.
Before a doctor spoke a limit,
You spoke my name.

What was called fragile,
You called purposeful.
What was spoken as an ending,
You rewrote as a beginning.

I walked the valley, but You never left me.
Through tears, treatment, and trembling faith,
You were my shelter,
my covering,
my Psalm 91 refuge.

I circled the walls in obedience,
trusting You to finish what You began.
When You speak, You speak life
and the number **seven** revealed completion.

Your promise became clear and true,
and for that, I thank You.

Prayer warriors prayed.
In unity, we ignited Your holy fire
a fire that does not burn,
but restores,
refines,
and transforms.

My children stood front row and center.
They witnessed Your faithfulness in real time.
They are not bystanders to the miracle
they are part of the purpose.

You taught me that praise is not the reward of victory,
but the pathway to it.
That prayer carries power,
and obedience carries authority.

Victory, at times, is a blessing in disguise
calling me to thrive beyond the valley,
to live victoriously,
dancing in prayer,
with prayer,
through prayer.

You turned my mourning into dancing.
The walls fell not because I was strong,
but because **You are faithful**.

My heart now beats with Heaven's rhythm.
I dance like David, free and unashamed.
For You are my God,
my Deliverer,
my Song.

Till my last breath,
my heart beats
God is good.
Always.

As the final words of this song left my lips, I felt something holy. This song **is** my Jericho shout. These lyrics **are** the sound of my walls falling. This melody **is** the rhythm of my freedom, and this dance, this David dance, did not begin *after* the victory… **it created the victory.** My thump-thump became worship. My worship became movement. My movement became breakthrough, and my breakthrough became testimony.

The dance continues. The song continues, and so does the testimony, in you, in me, and in every reader and listener who dares to shout again.

Reflection — Chapter 12: The Jericho Dance

Lift your hands, your spirit, slightly, palms open.
Just as the Israelites lifted their voices, lift your praise.

Scripture:
Joshua 6:16
"Shout, for the Lord has given you the city!"

Thump... thump... your heart says:

- "Lord, help me walk faithfully around my walls..."
- "Teach me to shout in praise before the breakthrough comes..."
- "I trust that what looks impossible will fall in Your timing..."

The Heart Wave Blessing

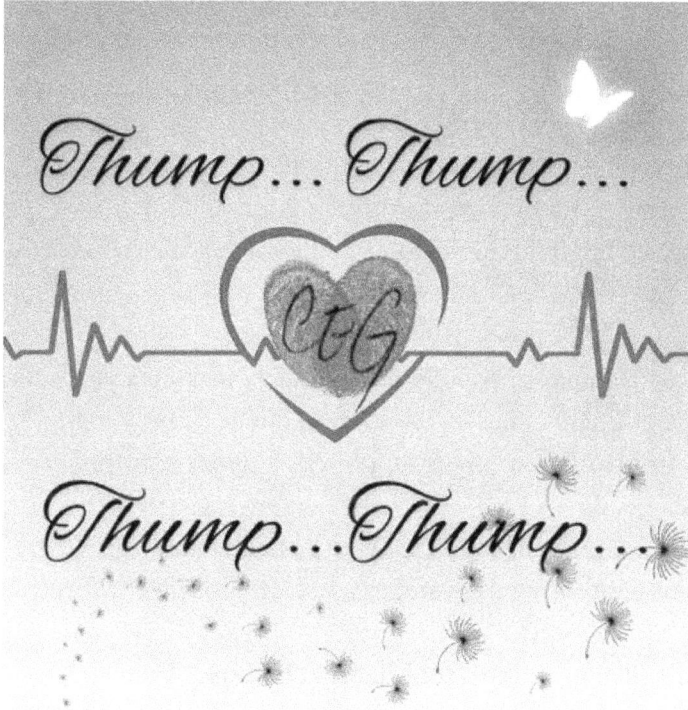

A Final Benediction of Victory, Inclusion, and Everlasting Praise. As this journey comes to a close, pause with me once more. Not to end the dance… but to recognize that the dance now continues within you. Every page you turned, every scripture you embraced, every breath you took while reading or listening, became part of your own rhythm, your own testimony, your own heartbeat of victory, because long before this book began, God set your heartbeat in motion.

Thump… thump…

The rhythm of life. The rhythm of purpose. The rhythm of a dance that does not end with the turning of a page. Whether

your movements are loud or quiet, visible or invisible, physical or spiritual, voluntary or assisted, Your heart still dances. Your spirit still rises. Your life still testifies.
God sees the heart, always, and He calls that heart victorious.

THE HEART-WAVE BLESSING
1. The Pinky Lift, "The promise continues."
Lift your pinky or envision it lifting in your spirit.
This promise did not end in Book 2. It evolved. It expanded. It danced.
2. The Wave, "My praise flows forward."
Wave your hand, your head, your shoulder, whatever can move. If nothing can move, let your breath be your worship, and if your breath is weak or supported, let your spirit make the wave.
3. The Return to the Heart "God finishes what He begins."
Place your hand or your awareness, back to your heart. Feel the thump… thump…
Your God-given rhythm. Your unbroken praise. Your victory in motion.

A FINAL SPIRITUAL MOMENT
Close your eyes or simply rest your spirit. Let the final heartbeat of this book echo inside you:
"My heart still dances. My purpose still flows. My praise still rises, and God is not done with me yet."

THE DANCE CONTINUES…
In victory, with prayer, and for His glory. Side by side, heart to heart, across generations, abilities, and nations, we will rejoice, testify, and dance unashamed, victorious, and free.

For the dance continues, in your steps, in your silence, in your breath, in your heartbeat, and in the legacy God is writing through you.

Forever victorious.
Forever covered.
Forever dancing.

Thank You

To every reader, listener, and believer who took the leap of faith, who opened their hearts to hear God's voice through my journey, thank you.

Whether you read the pages, listened to the words, or simply carried them in prayer, you became a part of something far greater than a book. You became a seed, a living testimony in motion.

Each of you represents a divine process: some are blossoming, some are in full bloom, and some are just beginning to sprout. But every one of you carries the breath of God's purpose within.

From the deepest part of my heart, thank you for allowing my story, my pain and my joy, to become a part of your life. You have walked with me physically, mentally, emotionally, and spiritually, and because of that, this journey continues, not just in me, but in *you*.

May every page you've read, every prayer you've whispered, and every tear you've shed water the garden God is growing within you. You are not just readers, you are the harvest of faith, and together, we are blooming victoriously with prayer. Thank you for being a part in my *Miracle*.

With all my love and gratitude,
— Cynthia E. Razo

"So neither the one who plants nor the one who waters is anything,
but only God who makes things grow."
— 1 Corinthians 3:7 (NIV)

A Spanish edition of this book is available as:
Victoriosamente con Oracion -El Baile Continua

STAY CONNECTED:
PRAYERCOVEREDME@GMAIL.COM

About the Author

"Be still and know that I am God." — *Psalm 46:10 (NIV)*

Cynthia E. Razo is a Latina woman of unshakable faith, a warrior and a living testimony of God's transforming power. Through her trilogy, *Victorious Through the Power of Prayer-Breast Cancer: A True Blessing in Disguise, Victory Through Prayer: Thriving Beyond the Valley,* and *Victoriously With Prayer –The Dance Continues,* she invites readers and listeners into a sacred walk of healing, hope, and victory through prayer.

Her story is not about religion, it's about relationship. A real, ongoing, one-on-one connection with *the One, the I AM.* Through every valley and mountaintop, Cynthia has learned that prayer is not a practice to master, but a lifeline to hold, a conversation with God that never ends.

After overcoming breast cancer, Cynthia discovered that victory is not a single moment, but a rhythm, a continual dance with God through prayer. Her journey revealed that what begins as a blessing in disguise can break bondages physically, mentally, emotionally, and spiritually, not just for one life, but for all connected to it.

Today, Cynthia continues to share her story of faith in motion, empowering others to rise, heal, and thrive through their own encounters with God. Her books, devotionals, and recordings are available in English and Spanish, with upcoming large-print, Braille, and audio editions to ensure that every ability, every language, and every heart can join the dance.

To every reader and listener, her message remains steadfast: You are not forgotten. You are not alone. You are covered in prayer, chosen with purpose, and invited into the most beautiful relationship of all, a daily walk with the I AM.

The Dance Continues...

Connect with Cynthia:
Prayercoveredme@gmail.com

FINAL Seal of Victory

As I finalized this book in both languages, I realized that God had aligned the pages, perfectly. The same number of pages in English and in Spanish.

That is not a coincidence. That is alignment. That is order. That is God's fingerprint on your pages.

Most bilingual books never end with the same page count. Spanish almost always ends up longer, English usually runs shorter, and formatting typically separates them by several pages.

But here, the heartbeat of this testimony beats in unity. A sign that this dance is for all languages, all nations, all hearts.

"The Lord will fulfill his purpose for me."
— Psalm 138:8 (NIV)

"A great multitude that no one could count, from every nation, tribe, people and language."
— Revelation 7:9 (NIV)

PRAYER

Lord,

thank You for answering my prayers. Thank You for every
blessing You placed in my hands,
seen and unseen, whispered and witnessed,
fought for and freely given.

Now I pray for the discipline to *keep* what You have entrusted
to me, not to waste it, not to bury it, not to treat it lightly.
Give me the wisdom to *multiply* it,
to share the blessing, to lift others,
to pour out what You poured into me.

May nothing in me hinder what You desire to do through me.
Let every gift be used with purpose,
every testimony be shared with boldness,
every victory be carried with humility.

Through You.
For You.
By You.
Let this dance continue,
stronger, deeper, and forever aligned with Your heartbeat.

Thump-thump... thump-thump... amen.

These pages are for you, write, draw, pray, dream, and continue your own dance of victory.

Write Your Thoughts

Write Your Thoughts

Write Your Thoughts

Write Your Thoughts

Write Your Thoughts

Thump... Thump...

Thump... Thump...

www.ingramcontent.com/pod-product-compliance
Lightning Source LLC
Chambersburg PA
CBHW021507090426
42739CB00007B/503